Other *Argyle Sweater* Books

The Argyle Sweater: A Cartoon Collection

50% Wool, 50% Asinine

Tastes Like Chicken: An Argyle Sweater Treasury

An *Argyle Sweater* **Collection by Scott Hilburn**

**Andrews McMeel
Publishing, LLC**

Kansas City • Sydney • London

The Argyle Sweater is distributed internationally by Universal Uclick.

Puns of Steel copyright © 2011 by Scott Hilburn. All rights reserved. Printed in China. No part of this book may be used or reproduced in any manner whatsoever without written permission except in the case of reprints in the context of reviews.

Andrews McMeel Publishing, LLC
an Andrews McMeel Universal company
1130 Walnut Street, Kansas City, Missouri 64106

www.andrewsmcmeel.com
www.theargylesweater.com

11 12 13 14 15 TEN 10 9 8 7 6 5 4 3 2 1

ISBN: 978-1-4494-0105-4

Library of Congress Control Number: 2010940192

ATTENTION: SCHOOLS AND BUSINESSES

Andrews McMeel books are available at quantity discounts with bulk purchase for educational, business, or sales promotional use. For information, please e-mail the Andrews McMeel Publishing Special Sales Department:
specialsales@amuniversal.com

To Maddie and Emma

BEATRICE WISHED HER HUSBAND WAS AROUND TO HAVE "THE TALK" WITH THEIR MATURING SON. THEN SHE REMEMBERED HIS ABSENCE WAS HER FAULT.

ARIEL PREPARES FOR HER BIG DATE

HEY, THAT'S NOT HIS LINE! COOKIES! HE'S SUPPOSED TO SAY, "ME WANT COOKIES!" WHOEVER HEARD OF THE INSULIN MONSTER??

BUDDHIST PHOTO ALBUMS

EZRA'S PURCHASE OF AN OFF-BRAND GPS DEVICE MEANT HE'D NEVER GET THE CHANCE TO MAKE HIS HORSE DRINK.

All the King's horses and all the King's men, couldn't restore the paint on the royal vehicle again.

MIDAS OFTEN FACED TOUGH DECISIONS.

TRUTH BE TOLD, STANLEY DIDN'T EVEN LIKE BASKETBALL, DESPITE ALWAYS BEING PICKED FIRST.

AMY'S HOPES THAT KYLE MIGHT POP THE QUESTION QUICKLY FADED AS THEY ARRIVED AT THE RESTAURANT.

AFTER MONTHS OF OBSERVATION, JEFFRIES AND CALLAHAN CONCLUDE THAT THE PRIMATES' MATING RITUALS WEREN'T UNLIKE THAT OF HUMANS.

15

THE CHAMELEON: MASTER OF DISGUISE

17

I KNOW THE SHAKESPEARE FAMILY HAS A RICH TRADITION OF CARPENTRY, BUT THE WOODSHOP CLASS IS FULL. THE ONLY ELECTIVE I STILL HAVE OPEN IS A CREATIVE-WRITING CLASS.

COUNSELOR

LI'L BILL MEETS DESTINY

THAT WAS COLONEL MUSTARD. HE'D LIKE A MOP, SOME BLEACH AND SEVERAL LARGE TRASH BAGS BROUGHT TO THE CONSERVATORY RIGHT AWAY.

BEFORE

AFTER

THE IMPACT OF THE STIMULUS PACKAGE WAS SUBTLE AT FIRST

19

JACK VISITS THE EMERGENCY ROOM

DORA THE EXTORTER

22

When alcohol and gimmicky restaurants collide.

PIONEER FIRE DRILLS

24

BLOCKBUSTER BOOK ADAPTATIONS GONE WRONG

25

Though less threatening than its deadlier cousin, beachgoers often try to avoid the swarms of Bach's jellyfish.

Upon clicking her heels and uttering the magic phrase, Dorothy unexpectedly suffers a concussion.

IT BECAME INCREASINGLY DIFFICULT FOR THE CAPTAIN TO REWARD HIS CREW AND STILL MAINTAIN HIS FEROCIOUS REPUTATION.

DIRTY MARTINI

EMMETT HAD A FAR MORE DIFFICULT TIME EXPLAINING THE HALTER TOP.

31

I DON'T KNOW WHAT HAPPENED IN THERE, STANLEY... BUT I'VE COMPLETELY LOST THE URGE TO EAT. I MEAN IT- I FEEL STUFFED! SUPPOSED TO COME BACK RIGHT BEFORE THANKSGIVING FOR A FOLLOW-UP THOUGH.
DR. CARVER'S WEIGHT-LOSS HYPNOSIS CLINIC
STOVE TOP
SCOTT HILBURN

DO NOT PRESS
SCOTT HILBURN
ULTIMATELY, WYATT'S CURIOSITY GOT THE BETTER OF HIM.

SCOTT HILBURN
ONCE ASHORE, THE PROFESSOR AND THE 'ISLAND OF WOMEN' DWELLERS EACH HAVE THEIR OWN IDEAS AND EXPECTATIONS.

HOW NON-FLYING SQUIRRELS TRAVEL

34

FRANK AND BYRON WERE ABOUT TO LEARN THAT THE ONE THING THESE ANIMALS DISLIKED MORE THAN BEING SURPRISED BY HUMANS WAS BEING HUMILIATED BY THEM.

... SO, I SAYS, "SHOOT HIM ONE MORE TIME JUST TO BE SURE," AND JIM SAYS, "I GOT HIM!" SO, I SAYS, "JUST ONCE MORE TO BE SURE," AND AGAIN HE SAYS, "I GOT HIM!" SO, I SAYS, "OKAY. LET'S GET A PICTURE WITH YOUR HEAD IN HIS MOUTH."... YOU KNOW - LIKE ONE OF THEM LION TAMER POSES ...

I KNOW... CRAZY, RIGHT? I MEAN, WHAT'RE THE ODDS OF GETTING **BOTH** HANDS STUNG? SWELLING SHOULD SUBSIDE IN A FEW DAYS... ANYHOW, LET'S GET ON WITH THE EXAM, I GUESS.

ANDY PINTER AND HIS ANT FARM	FRANKIE BOMGARTEN AND HIS FLEA CIRCUS
SARA EFFERMAN AND HER SEA MONKEY HABITAT	LOUIE HOROWITZ AND HIS LICE SANCTUARY

UNPOPULAR KIDS ON SHOW AND TELL DAY

39

INSIDE THE MIND OF YOUR CRAZY EX-BOYFRIEND

ALMOST AS QUICKLY AS IT HAD STARTED, THE FOOD FIGHT ENDED.

HER FLAG PROJECT NEAR COMPLETION, BETSY ROSS PONDERS A PATRIOTIC WAY TO REPRESENT THE COLONIES WHEN INSPIRATION SUDDENLY STRIKES HER.

YEAH, LOOKS LIKE WE FINALLY CAUGHT THAT PEEPING TOM. NEED TO RUN HIS LICENSE. LAST NAME? UHH... "GEICO." FIRST NAME?... "THE MONEY YOU COULD BE SAVING."

THE TEEN YEARS OF A RED DELICIOUS.

TRAGEDY ANN

Their marriage in jeopardy, Strawberry Shortcake and Billy Bob Banana Bread seek therapy.

53

JAMES BOND: SENIOR YEARS

So, in your gown and glass slipper, you dash from the ball, *before midnight*, only to find your carriage missing... No further questions, your honor. Now I'd like to call the defendant to the stand—Peter Peter Pumpkin Eater.

THE UNTOLD HISTORY OF GENERAL TSO

A SIMPLE MISUNDERSTANDING BY A YOUNG FRANK SINATRA WOULD LEAD TO A FORTUITOUS CAREER MOVE

THE TATTOOS HE ONCE THOUGHT CLEVER, ARTIE NOW REGRETTED.

TO MOTHERS, HE WAS A MIRACLE WORKER. TO DR. WEXLER, IT WAS JUST ANOTHER DAY AT WORK DELIVERING BABIES.

59

LIKE OTHER LEGENDARY BRITS, YOUNG ERIC CLAPTON DISCOVERED HIS DESTINY QUITE BY ACCIDENT.

I JUST SAW TWO TARANTULAS CLIMB INTO YOUR SLEEPING BAG — AND A RACCOON STOLE YOUR SHOE... HE'S OVER BEHIND THAT TREE.

...AND WHEN LARRY LIFTED THE ROCK, THERE IT WAS: THE LEAST-LIKED MEMBER OF THE ANIMAL KINGDOM — THE TATTLE SNAKE.

ON THE EVE OF HIS EPIC DEFEAT BY "DEEP BLUE," GARRY KASPAROV AWOKE TO AN OMINOUS WARNING.

THE TEAM ORIGINALLY CALLED THEMSELVES THE FANTASTIC 5, UNTIL THE GROUP DECIDED THAT TUBA TIM'S PERFORMANCE WASN'T SO FANTASTIC.

ORNITHOLOGICAL STUDIES PERFORMED BY DR. WORTHINGTON PROVED DEFINITIVELY THAT 4 OUT OF 5 BIRDS PREFER APPLES TO WINDOWS.

OKAY, BOYS... PAPER ALREADY BEAT THESE GUYS ONCE — AND WE BEAT PAPER LAST WEEK. WITHOUT GETTING OVERCONFIDENT, IF WE STICK TO OUR GAME, WE SHOULD HAVE NO PROBLEMS.

Do it, GROK! Do it!

MAMMOTH TIPPING WAS THE MOST FATAL OF PRIMITIVE TEEN ACTIVITIES.

DARN... SO CLOSE.

MULLINS VACUUM CO.

MULL VACU

CHET BLOWS ANOTHER SALE

PICKUP!

DING!

LOOK, GRANDPA! EVERY TIME A BELL RINGS, AN ANGEL GETS HIS WINGS!

CIRCA 1995: JIMMY STEWART ARRIVES FOR LUNCH WITH HIS GRANDDAUGHTER, WHEN LIFE SUDDENLY IMITATES ART.

65

FOR THE THIRD TIME IN AS MANY MORNINGS, AMY STARTS HER DAY IN A GOOD MOOD, WHILE TED AGAIN WAKES UP ON THE WRONG SIDE OF THE BED.

CONRAD GREW TO RESENT THE FOUR CALLING BIRDS HIS TRUE LOVE GAVE TO HIM.

HEY, C'MON – IT'S OKAY, MAN. I'LL CONFESS TO THE ROBBERY IF YOU'LL JUST STOP CRYING.

THE CONTROVERSIAL BUT EFFECTIVE GOOD COP/SAD COP ROUTINE.

COME TO PAPA!

THE ARGYLE SWEATER PRESENTS:
Rejected Applications for the Ninth Wonder of the World

The Porchlight of Alexandria, Va.

The Singing Waiter of West Hollywood

The Shoe Lifts of Tom Cruise

6 INCHES +

The Beard Comb of Wolf Blitzer

Prince Charles' Earmuffs

The Cheesecake Factory's Chocolate Cake

No longer a child, Maureen is excited to experience her first holiday dinner at the big table.

YOUR MOTHER ALWAYS GIVES THE WORST HOUSEWARMING GIFTS.

WELCOME HOME!

HEY, SWEETIE, I'M NOT SURE IF IT WAS SOMETHING I ATE OR SOMETHING I SAT ON... EITHER WAY, I'VE KINDA HAD A BLOWOUT. CAN YOU BRING ME A SPARE?

TIMMY ACE 3

MICHELIN

LESSER-KNOWN ANIMAL PRINTS

TROY'S RENOWNED GYMNASTICS TEAM HAD NEVER BEFORE RECEIVED A GIFT OF SUCH GENEROSITY.

AFTER A FEW COCKTAILS, GROK MAKES THE TRAGIC MISTAKE OF GETTING BEHIND THE WHEEL.

REJECTED FAST FOOD PROMOTIONS

DQ "GUESS THE MEAT AND IT'S FREE TO EAT!"

SONIC "C'MON, PUSH OUR BUTTONS!"

LONG JOHN SILVER'S "TRY OUR COD PIECES"

KFT KENTUCKY FRIED TOFU "HEY P.E.T.A., EAT THIS!"

W "NEW! FRY ON A STICK!"

THE ARGYLE SWEATER PRESENTS: The Worst Selling Books of the 1980's–1990's

LET ME TEACH YOU TO ACT by Philip Michael Thomas

FOREVER MARRIAGES BY ROSEANNE & TOM ARNOLD

TOO LEGIT FOR SUZE ORMAN   MERRILL LYNCH CAN'T TOUCH THIS! Budgeting & Finance with M.C. Hammer

Teal: THE COLOR OF THE 21ST CENTURY

The Straight and Narrow by Bobby Brown

What I'm Talking About BY TODD BRIDGES

80

81

WHILE HIS NEMESIS ORDERED A SCONE, LEVI WAS AGAIN SAVED BY THE F.B.I.'S HIGH-BUDGET WITNESS PROTECTION PROGRAM-ISSUED DISGUISES.

JOHN HANCOCK'S LATER YEARS TAINTED HIS LEGACY

83

85

ANOTHER UNSUCCESSFUL MAIL CARRIER

NEIL ARMSTRONG READIES FOR THE MOON LANDING

ROMULUS AND REMUS' CONTRACTOR DISPUTE

AMATEUR VAMPIRE HUNTERS

UNHOLY MACKEREL

91

AN EXPERIENCED AUTHOR, GIGI DEVAULT WAS NO STRANGER TO WRITER'S BLOCK. THIS WAS, HOWEVER, HER FIRST ENCOUNTER WITH THE EQUALLY DISRUPTIVE CINDER BLOCK.

FIRST HE WARMS OUR BOWL, NOW HE'S FEEDING US... AND YOU THOUGHT HE WASN'T FRIENDLY.

PAVLOV'S DAUGHTER,
NEVER MARRIED

THE MOST EMBARRASSING DAY IN THE
HISTORY OF THE SWISS ARMY.

EARLY VERSIONS OF THE NEW YEAR'S EVE BALL DROP PROVED LESS POPULAR AMONG REVELERS.

105

HE WAS NEVER ALL THAT GOOD AT CHASING CARS. UNFORTUNATELY FOR HARLEY, HE WAS EVEN LESS ADEPT AT READING.

THE PRYING MANTIS

LADY GODIVA'S HIGH SCHOOL NIGHTMARE

There they are! Get th— wait... wait... They're already trapped in some kind of invisible box... let's move along.

Obi-Wan and Yoda again evade capture thanks to the seldom-used Jedi mime trick.

No, no, no, Fielder! If I've said it once, I've said it a thousand times— use the whisk! I hate to beat a dead horse but, well... it /s our job.

GLUE

Whoa, whoa, whoa, kid. You can't come in here throwin' that label around. There's no pattern here, no prior victims— nothin'! Sure, it's tragically malicious, but it ain't no serial killer.

DOE-TO-DOE SALESMAN

AFTER 39 YEARS AND 11 MONTHS OF STUBBORNLY WANDERING THE DESERT, MOSES' WIFE DECIDES TO ASK FOR DIRECTIONS TO THE PROMISED LAND.

TRUEMAN DEWAYNE LAFAYETTE:
COLLECTOR OF THE IMAGINARY

DANCES WITH WOLVES' LESSER-KNOWN SIBLINGS

BOOGIES WITH ELK

FLIRTS WITH COUGARS

FERTILIZES WITH BEARS

RUNS WITH ELEPHANTS

LEAPFROGS WITH UNICORNS

STAN

CHET SEES AN OLD FLAME

OUTBACK TASTE TESTS CONFIRM THAT 4 OUT OF 5 CROCS PREFER PEPSI KOALA OVER COCA KOALA